floored

floored

Furnish your floors: 25 stunning surface solutions

Catherine Tully

Photography by Graham Rae

southwater

This edition is published by Southwater

Southwater is an imprint of
Anness Publishing Limited
Hermes House
88–89 Blackfriars Road
London SE1 8HA
tel. 020 7401 2077
fax 020 7633 9499

Distributed in the USA by
Anness Publishing Inc.
27 West 20th Street
Suite 504
New York
NY 10011
fax 212 807 6813

Distributed in the UK by
The Manning Partnership
251–253 London Road East
Batheaston
Bath BA1 7RL
tel. 01225 852 727
fax 01225 852 852

Distributed in Australia by
Sandstone Publishing
Unit 1
360 Norton Street
Leichhardt
New South Wales 2040
tel. 02 9560 7888
fax 02 9560 7488

1 3 5 7 9 10 8 6 4 2

Publisher: Joanna Lorenz
Photographer: Graham Rae
Designer: Caroline Reeves

PUBLISHER'S NOTE
The publishers have made every effort to ensure that all instructions are accurate and safe, and cannot accept
any liability for any resulting injury, damage or loss to persons or property however it may arise. If in any
doubt about the correct procedure to follow for any home improvements tasks seek professional advice.

Previously published as *Floor Furnishing*

CONTENTS

INTRODUCTION

*Floors are the very base of your living place and are often the first thing you
have to replace or renew when moving into a home. In previous years, people
wanted floors to last a lifetime. The major consideration was durability and home-
owners spent as much as they could afford on it. Now we are much more mobile and
our homes are often seen as short- or medium-term accommodation, because of work
or the planned growth of the family. We also change our furnishings more often,
so today's requirement is for chic and inexpensive flooring that has instant
design impact.*

*Contemporary flooring can be a little more daring and fun, and use lighter and less
expensive materials. If in doubt about a room's final use or colour scheme, a beautiful,
neutral floor will allow you to alter either. The scale of a room is also important: large
patterns are seen to best advantage only in large rooms with the minimum of furniture.
However, floors are often the main feature of halls and passages, even more so when seen
from an upper landing. In this situation, go for a really eye-catching floor treatment.
Practicality is also important. Consider whether the area is going to be exposed to water,
as in a bathroom, or to heavy wear, as in a kitchen, and whether durability is
paramount or whether a more whimsical surface would suffice. But above all, choose
projects that appeal to you and that will give you floors you will
enjoy creating and living with.*

PAINTED FLOORS

Above: Use different shades of wood stain for a restful effect. Here, the border of oak leaves was reverse-stencilled, then the details of the leaves were applied freehand.

If you are lucky enough to inherit a house that has naturally beautiful wooden floors, you may wish to do no more than add a decorative border. If the floor has been waxed or varnished it will be necessary to remove this layer first with a wood stripper or sander. Modern paints allow for a multitude of effects, but don't overlook wood stains, which can be used in combination to produce subtle effects that are eminently suitable for a classic country home.

Stencilling has a folksy image that people associate with country cottages, but in reality, this is one of the most versatile of treatments, as well as being one of the simplest. Either buy one of the many stencilling kits available, or, if you are feeling more adventurous, photocopy a favourite motif, stick the photocopy to a sheet of acetate and cut out the stencil. Bold, geometric motifs are the easiest for novices both to cut and paint. If you are more experienced, you might like to try designs derived from flower shapes or more elaborate flounces.

When using colour, remember a few basic principles: neutral tones always work well together but can be boring; complementary colours (red and green, yellow and violet) have tremendous zing but can be wearing on the eye; different tones of the same colour, possibly with sharp accents in a much lighter or darker tone, are restful. Black and white are always good together, a classic combination for halls, kitchens and bathrooms. Some of the paint effects in this book may look complicated but if you follow the instructions carefully you will soon realize how very easy they are. Always remember that no paint effect need be permanent. If you tire of the design, strip the floor down and start again. Similarly, any signs of wear and tear that begin to show can be touched up. Varnishing is important. Once you have decided whether you want a matt or gloss finish, apply several coats of varnish to build up a really hard-wearing layer and make sure the room is well-ventilated. Some varnishes are available that have been specially formulated for floors, and though these are more expensive than conventional varnishes, generally only two or three coats are needed.

Above: Stamps are an easy way to decorate and the variety now available ready-made is enormous. Use them for a simple but decorative edging, to give a hand-made quality that is totally in keeping with the natural wood floor.

Left: If you don't want, or can't afford, a patterned carpet, and your wooden floor is in good condition, create a wholly unique and individual look, with just as much colour and interest as a carpet, with stencilling. You can be as bold or as subtle as you like.

RUGS

If you don't want to embark on a complete change of flooring, or while you're still making up your mind about changing the floor, rugs can disguise faults, add new colour and textural interest, provide warmth and softness for your feet and help to soften the acoustics of a room with a lot of hard surfaces. They are available in as many sizes, shapes, textures, colours and styles as the imaginations of home-owners can conceive: some of the most precious silk rugs and carpets from Persia, Turkey and the Orient are extremely valuable but equal ethnic style can be found in inexpensive street-market bargains. Classic and traditional styles are available to suit period interiors of every age and style, but superb modern designs, which make focal points in the same way as a striking abstract painting hung over a mantelpiece, are equally easy to find. Moving into making your own opens up a limitless range of style options, provided you are not afraid to be bold.

Above: The classic interpretation: a perfectly simple, textured wool rug on a beautiful wooden floor. The simplicity and purity of the rug perfectly set off the subtle variations of colour found in the floor boards.

Right: This isn't a traditional rug, but it would be at home in either a country-cottage-style or modern interior. The calm colour scheme and the invocation of heavenly tranquillity make this especially suitable for a bedroom or study. It's unmistakably hand-made but far from lacking in sophistication.

Above: This is a classic folk-art-style rug.

Above: Unmistakably rustic, this rug would make an instant focal point.

Left: Made with a traditional hooking technique, this bath mat uses seashore colours, to create a modern interpretation of the kind of home-made rug that was once to be found in bathrooms everywhere.

TILES

Above: Flagstones and tiles have long been popular, not just in cottages and farmhouses but in larger country houses too. These are laid in a traditional Victorian style, but if your home is not of that period, you could make a simple, modern pattern to equally dramatic effect.

Tiles are one of the most expensive forms of flooring, but they look beautiful and are very hard-wearing. Because of all these factors, be prepared to spend quite a lot of time before you actually lay the floor evaluating the many different tiles that are available. Don't be afraid to spend money if you find tiles you could really die for. Choose a cheaper alternative, and you may live to regret it. The terracotta tiles that are imported from countries in the Mediterranean and South America look gorgeous with their sunburnt colours. Hunting round architectural salvage yards can often yield an entire Victorian floor, but if you have no luck, most DIY stores sell a wide range of alternatives. If you have the patience, a mosaic floor can look stunning, particularly where there is an open space and not much furniture, in a hallway, for example.

Right: Originally imported and copied from countries with a history of terracotta tiles, these are now available in such a vast variety that you can create a very individual floor, just by choosing different finishes and sizes.

Above: The elegance of marble is available quite cheaply now, particularly in this single grey colour: most DIY stores stock it. Though slightly daunting to cut and lay, marble tiles are the perfect cool, elegant solution in areas where you are likely to have damp, such as bathrooms.

Above: A bathroom and kitchen standard for most of this century, ceramic tiles don't have to be boring. This interesting design is an eye-catching focal point in its own right, for an otherwise empty area such as a corridor. Combining elements of Islamic style, and with more than a hint of the mosaics that graced Roman buildings, this is a modern and humorous interpretation, perfectly illustrating the sheer versatility of tiles as a decorative medium for floors.

Above: Wooden flooring materials tend to make use of the same principles as tiles for their aesthetic effect: the combination of interlocking shapes and natural textures is here enhanced by the addition of the cool, clean metal of the heating grilles – a lesson in combining form and function.

DECORATIVE SKIRTINGS

Above: This is a very game skirting, which would brighten up most rooms and would be an appropriate companion to, say, a striped floor or a plain floor which boasted a rather zany rug.

At the most mundane level, skirtings tidy up the area between the floor and the walls, and have the practical function of covering up any pipes and keeping out the draughts, but they should not be neglected, as they supply the necessary visual tie between the two surfaces.

In the past most people were content to do no more than give their skirting boards the occasional lick of gloss paint, but these days no-one need feel bound to stick to the old conventions. In a room decorated in soothing neutrals that is to be furnished perhaps with just a few very beautiful pieces of antique furniture, for instance, mimic the patina of the wood by coating the skirting boards with matching woodstain. This can then be varnished to a gloss, matt or satin finish; whichever you think is most appropriate. If you don't mind the extra work, you could try sanding the last coat of varnish, then polishing with the same wax that you usually use on the furniture.

In another situation, you might prefer to be as bold and imaginative with your skirtings as you are with walls and floors. It would be quite a fun idea to brighten an otherwise soberly decorated room with a zanily patterned skirting, a bit like wearing a jazzy tie with a dark business suit, for example; or stick to the colour scheme you have already opted for, perhaps by using a few of the colours in a more restricted space. A montage effect can also be fun, particularly if you can pick up a motif from the curtains, a cushion or some other item in the room. Cut suitable pictures from a magazine or catalogue, or photocopy a favourite image several times. You can leave the images black and white or colour them with inks using an artist's brush. Stick them to the skirting carefully with wallpaper paste, wipe off the excess and then varnish several times.

Top right: This is a very whimsical way to give your room an instant air of fun. The subjects for montages are endless: the only limitation is how good you are at cutting out fine motifs and, since there is no wear and tear, you could afford to run riot by telling whole stories on your skirting: try a poem or a picture-and-word series running round the skirting in a cloakroom.

Middle right: Add a note of colour by painting the skirting in a contrasting colour, such as this distressed green, which still harmonizes perfectly with natural wood tones and textures.

Bottom right: For a natural wood floor, choose a complementary tone for the wood stain for the skirting. Combined with plain neutral-colour walls, this is the classic treatment for modern and period-style interiors where the furnishings are the star of the show.

EMBELLISHED SKIRTINGS

Above: This looks like something left over from a medieval doorway or at least from the Wild West. Add really strong texture with metal studs: you could even apply pieces of leather, too, and make a heavy-metal and biker-influenced skirting.

If the surface of a skirting board strikes you as too flat and dull, give it a bit of texture by adding one of the embellishments suggested here. DIY stores are full of decorative beading and mouldings that are intended for use on MDF furniture but which can equally well be applied to skirtings (using the adhesive recommended by the manufacturer). It is easier to paint this before applying, then allow it to dry, rather than painting it *in situ*. But don't let your imagination stop there. Experiment, for instance, with rope patterns on a flat surface. When you hit on one you like, draw the shape in pencil on the skirting, then follow this with a line of glue. Allow this to become tacky, then press the rope into place. Either leave the rope in its natural colour, dye it or spray it with metallic paint, for a real touch of Versailles splendour.

Some of the floor treatments in this book can be adapted easily to skirting boards. The studded floor idea, for instance, is equally stunning when applied to the vertical surface. Or try cutting self-adhesive rubber mats into geometric shapes for a liquorice allsort look. Whatever you do, make sure your skirting boards are really "off the wall".

Right: Here, self-stick rubber mats were cut into wacky, liquorice-allsorts-style embellishments; alternatively, play noughts and crosses or just make the most of the texture, painting the rubber all one colour.

Top right: Rope gives wonderful three-dimensional effects to your skirtings. Again, because the area doesn't suffer much wear and tear, it could be left au naturel *for a back-to-nature look or painted gold or all white for a touch of operatic diva style.*

Middle right: If you like a quirky, witty element in a décor scheme, this idea, which will certainly bamboozle visitors at first glance, is for you. Wooden mouldings come in such a variety of types that this rope moulding, coupled with painted holes, is just one of many trompe l'oeil *effects you can achieve.*

Bottom right: An elaborate paint effect here; a lightly marbled skirting is embellished with gold-painted beading for a classy but divinely decadent look.

BUTTERFLY MONTAGE

Surrealism and the work of Ernst, Escher, Fornasetti and Magritte inspire the use of unusual yet familiar objects in designs for montages. This butterfly floor could just as easily have been made using motifs of flowers, boats or chairs. Strong lines are important and books of wonderful line drawings, are available. Lay the motifs down in an ordered pattern, rather than randomly. Here the design suggests the flight pattern of butterflies.

YOU WILL NEED
- ◆ light-coloured emulsion paint
- ◆ paint roller
- ◆ motifs
- ◆ craft knife
- ◆ self-healing cutting mat
- ◆ wallpaper paste
- ◆ paintbrushes
- ◆ indelible felt-tipped pen or fine artist's brush and oil-based paints
- ◆ matt varnish

1 Make sure your floor is completely smooth. If necessary, lay a hardboard or marine-plywood floor (*see Techniques*). Paint the floor a light colour so that the motifs will show up. Photocopy your chosen image(s) in at least seven sizes from small to large.

2 Using a craft knife, carefully cut out every image.

3 Decide on the positions of your images and stick them in place with wallpaper paste.

4 Add remaining fine details with a fine artist's brush and/or an indelible felt-tipped pen. Finish by applying at least six coats of varnish to be sure of its durability (some acrylic varnishes dry very quickly) or apply a specially strong floor varnish.

PASTEL STRIPES

Stripes are having a revival, and can transform a room, adding a light playfulness on a minimal budget.

For maximum effect, keep your furnishings light and funky and add bright patches of unexpected colour with small objects such as vases, chairs, flowers, and so on. The alternating colours also allow you to bring in different cushions and curtains for different seasons. For a child's room, substitute bold reds, blues, yellows and greens for these pastel colours.

YOU WILL NEED
◆ masking tape
◆ pencil (optional)
◆ eggshell matt paint: lemon, pastel blue, pink and green
◆ paintbrushes
◆ matt varnish

1 Prepare your floorboards by securing any loose boards and sanding them (*see Techniques*). Bear in mind that the paint emphasizes any faults in the wood, so repair and sand the floor thoroughly. Test your colour combination on a separate board.

2 Mask along the edges of every alternate board. You may find it helpful to indicate your colour choice on each board in pencil, so you don't lose track of the repeat order.

3 Starting with the lightest colour, paint all the boards inbetween the ones edged with the masking tape. Leave the paint to dry then remove the tape and replace it on the painted boards. Paint all the boards in this way.

4 Finally, when the stripes are completely dry, apply two or three coats of varnish to seal.

PISTACHIO-SHELL BORDER

In India and the east, decoration on floors and walls is as varied as the materials available. The floors of temples and shrines are often intricately patterned with everyday natural objects. Taking this as inspiration, use seeds, shells, stones, bits of china, mirror fragments or anything else you can think of, as long as it has a flat surface. In these hot countries, soft sandals or bare feet are the norm; in this country, restrict your flooring with shells to the rooms in which you don't normally wear shoes or to areas of low wear. You can fill in just a small area or, if you've a great fondness for pistachio nuts, fill in your whole border. A simple corner measuring about 1.2 x 1.2m/4 x 4 ft takes about 3kg/7lb of unshelled pistachio nuts.

YOU WILL NEED

- ◆ cream emulsion paint
- ◆ paint roller
- ◆ paint-mixing tray
- ◆ ruler
- ◆ pencil
- ◆ masking tape
- ◆ blue acrylic eggshell paint
- ◆ paintbrushes
- ◆ PVA glue
- ◆ pistachio shells
- ◆ natural sponge
- ◆ eggshell emulsion paint: peach, cream and pale blue

2 Measure and draw out your straight borders and edge them with masking tape. Draw your curved shapes straight on to the floor freehand or using a traced shape.

1 Make sure your floor surface is sound, dry and level; cover with hardboard or marine-plywood (*see Techniques*), if necessary. Apply a base coat of cream emulsion.

3 Fill in the lines with blue paint.

4 Apply a generous amount of PVA glue to the blue areas, working on a small area at a time. The PVA should be quite thick. Apply pistachio shells to the PVA, working on the fine areas first. You may find you need to grade the shells by size, in advance.

5 Once the PVA is completely clear and dry, apply blue paint over the shells and touch up any areas of cream paint that need it.

6 To paint the area inside the border, start by sponging on the darkest colour (in the photograph, peach) randomly; cover the whole area all at once.

7 Allow to dry completely and then repeat, using a softer shade of the same colour (in the photograph, peach mixed with cream).

8 Allow to dry and then use the same technique to apply a new colour (in the photograph, pale blue) over it.

9 Seal the floor with watered-down PVA as recommended by the manufacturer; it should be quite thick over the shells. The whiteness will disappear as it dries, leaving a clear surface. Allow to dry completely.

BOARD GAME CARPET TILES

Along with lino tiles, carpet tiles are real winners in the practicality stakes. Almost unbeatable in areas that need to be hard-wearing and where children and their attendant wear and tear are concerned, carpet tiles have the single disadvantge that they never look like fitted carpet, no matter how well they are laid. Rather than fighting the fact that they come in non-fraying squares, make use of this very quality and create a fun floor-scape, such as this giant board game. Carpet tiles are very forgiving, allowing for slight discrepancies in cutting, and are very easy to replace if an area is damaged. A geometrical design is easiest; it is advisable to leave curves to the experts, but anything else, from a board game to the elegance of a painting by Mondrian, is accessible.

1 Measure your room and make sure that the floor is level and all protruding nails have been flattened. Any flat surface will accommodate the carpet tiles, whether it is marine-plywood, hardboard, floor boards or concrete.

2 Plan your design, on paper. Most rooms are not perfectly square or rectangular so leave room for an area of plain tiles to edge the pattern.

3 Measure the tiles, to determine the size of your pointed shapes and to work out how many tiles will be needed for your pattern. Consider the different weaves and nap of the carpet tiles and make them work to enhance your chosen plan. Using a white crayon or chinagraph pencil, draw the pattern on the reverse of your tiles.

4 With the metal ruler and a rigid-bladed knife, score along the marked lines. Don't attempt to cut the tile through completely in one action.

5 Starting at the top of the tile, cut down your scored lines. Do this on a solid surface and take extreme care in doing it.

6 Lay down a line of carpet tape and remove the backing. Cut all the tiles for one complete run and fit these first, rather than laying little bits at a time.

7 Stick your cut tiles in place, making sure not to pack them too tightly. Begin by making the whole of the checkered border. Then fill in, laying strips of carpet tape as you work. Tread the tiles down, uneven cuts will be unnoticeable.

Right: A chessboard would also make a good pattern for a floor.

STUDDED FLOOR

Create the look of the deck of a battleship, with studs at regular intervals painted in battleship grey; or leave the wood natural and the studs unpainted for a medieval banqueting hall effect. The studs are called "domes of silence", because they are designed to be used under chair legs to help chairs glide across the floor without noise. However, you could use any studs, with the proviso that they aren't sharp or liable to cause damage to shoes or furniture.

YOU WILL NEED

◆ pencil

◆ steel ruler or straight edge

◆ studs or "domes of silence"

◆ eraser

◆ acrylic varnish (optional)

◆ paintbrush (optional)

◆ tack hammer

◆ cloth, softwood block or carpet scrap

◆ wood glue (optional)

1 Decide on the spacing and pattern of the studs or domes. Draw diagonal grid lines in accordance with your design and mark with a little cross where each stud is to go. Rub out all markings, except the crosses.

2 If necessary, apply a couple of coats of acrylic varnish to the whole floor, to seal the wood.

3 Using a hammer and something soft, such as a folded cloth or softwood block, to prevent damage to the studs, hammer them in over the crosses. If you use domes of silence, which have relatively shallow teeth, hammer them in only half way to start with. Remove the domes, apply a little wood glue and then replace them and hammer them in all the way. This technique can be used on any decorative wooden floor.

STAMPS AND DRY BRUSH

Sometimes, where a room has unusual furnishings, it is good to give it a distinctive style, by making a statement on the walls or floor. Here, the busy look of dry brush strokes combines with the simplicity of Japanese characters. The result is a warm yet stylish look that makes a memorable room.

YOU WILL NEED

- ◆ calligraphy brush
- ◆ black ink
- ◆ paper
- ◆ scissors
- ◆ paper glue
- ◆ foam block
- ◆ craft knife
- ◆ cream, rust-coloured and white emulsion paint
- ◆ large and small paint roller
- ◆ dry paintbrush
- ◆ masking tape
- ◆ black and rust-coloured ink
- ◆ matt varnish

1 Paint your Japanese characters with the calligraphy brush first, following the examples shown in this project. Make photocopies of each design.

2 Cut the characters out roughly and glue one of each character to the foam. Keeping the knife at an angle, cut away all the white paper and the foam underneath it, to make a raised stamp.

3 Prepare the floor, hammering in any protruding nails, and make sure it is clean and dry. Give the whole floor a base coat of cream emulsion and allow to dry.

4 Using masking tape, mask off both edges of alternate boards

5 Draw a dry brush, dipped into a little neat rust paint, across the unmasked boards in a series of parallel strokes, allowing the base coat to show through in places.

6 Repeat this exercise with white paint, which softens the whole effect. Leave to dry, then repeat the procedure with both colours on the remaining boards.

7 Plan your design of Japanese characters, using spare photocopies of the characters, roughly cut out.

8 Using a small roller, ink some of the stamps with black ink.

9 Replace some of the photocopies with black stamped characters.

10 Repeat, using the rust-coloured ink. Seal well with matt varnish and allow to dry.

PHOTOCOPY MONTAGE

This effect is reminiscent of the wonderful painted floors of European palaces. Few of us can afford to commission frescoes and floor painting but you might still aspire to a home decorated fit for Marie Antoinette. Using photocopied images can turn these dreams into reality. Choose any theme: the photograph shows a composition of landscapes, but architectural drawings, classical motifs, such as columns, garden urns and statues or even still-lifes of fruit, vegetables and china, could be made into successful montages. Using the same techniques, create a totally modern feeling using colour photocopies of, say, flower heads; instead of stencilling the borders, add freehand leaves and scrolls if you are skilled.

YOU WILL NEED

◆ cream and green eggshell emulsion paint
◆ paintbrushes
◆ photocopied images
◆ long metal ruler
◆ craft knife
◆ self-healing cutting mat
◆ artist's watercolour or acrylic paints
◆ gum arabic tape (if necessary)
◆ pencil
◆ masking tape
◆ acetate sheet
◆ bleed-proof paper (such as tracing paper)
◆ green stencil paint
◆ stencil brush
◆ wallpaper paste
◆ matt varnish

1 Starting with a well-prepared hard-board or marine-plywood floor (*see Techniques*), paint on an undercoat of cream eggshell paint, followed by a top coat. Allow to dry completely.

2 Experiment with images at different sizes and settle on an arrangement that looks good on your floor. Trim the images so that you are left with just the picture.

3 If your images are black and white, use watercolour or acrylic paints to put soft washes of colour over the prints. You may need to stretch the paper, using gum arabic tape, depending on the quality of the paper (test a small area first).

4 Arrange the photocopies on the floor and plan and draw out the borders. Mask off the boxes where the photcopies will go, with masking tape.

5 Paint between the lines of masking tape with green eggshell paint. When the paint is almost dry, gently peel off the masking tape, to reveal crisply defined borders beneath.

6 For the stencilled borders, photo-copy the template at the back of the book to the required size, then place over the acetate sheet and cut it out with a craft knife on the cutting mat. For the smaller pattern areas, mask off unneeded elements of your stencil using bleed-proof paper (such as tracing paper) and masking tape.

7 Apply the stencil to the floor with masking tape and stipple the stencilled border areas with green paint.

8 Spread the photocopies on the back with wallpaper paste and position them on the floor. Varnish the floor several times.

Opposite: Create a floor with the feel of an eighteenth-century European palace by combining a montage of photocopied images with decorative stencilling.

DECKING OR DUCKBOARDS

The Japanese bathhouse is the inspiration for this floor treatment, preventing pools of water from turning your bathroom into a skating rink and, at the same time, imparting the serenity of a Zen garden. In this project the duckboards form a pontoon or walkway across the bathroom, but you could also use sections and cut them around the bathroom fittings. Ready-made decking is also available in strips or squares.

YOU WILL NEED
- ◆ tape measure
- ◆ saw
- ◆ quadrant beading
- ◆ duckboards or decking
- ◆ drill with wood bit and pilot bit
- ◆ wood stain
- ◆ soft cloth
- ◆ paintbrush
- ◆ wood screws

1 Make sure you have a clean, level floor: cork tiles, wood and lino are all suitable. The existing floor will show through so if you want to change the colour, do so now! Measure and cut the two lengths of beading to the same length as the runners on the decking. Drill holes through these new runners.

2 Stain the two new long runners to the same colour as the duckboards.

3 Measure the distance between the runners on the duckboard.

4 Space the new runners at a distance that will allow the duckboard runners to slide between them, holding the duckboard steady but allowing it to be lifted up for cleaning. Screw in place by drilling through the subfloor, using the correct type of bit for the type of floor you have. Slide the duckboards or decking into place.

PARQUET

Good parquet is a very manageable kind of flooring. There are numerous patterns to be made from combining these wooden blocks. A good trick is to work out the pattern starting from the centre and make it as big a perfect square as you can; then lay a simple border to accommodate all the tricky outside edges. Parquet is often in oak but you could dye it with stain or varnish for a richer effect.

YOU WILL NEED

- ◆ pencil
- ◆ ridged spreader
- ◆ PVA floor adhesive
- ◆ parquet blocks
- ◆ timber length
- ◆ matt varnish
- ◆ paintbrush
- ◆ fine-grade sandpaper

1 Make sure your floor surface is clean, dry and level. Find your starting point as for laying floor tiles (*see Techniques*) and draw guidelines on the floor. Using a ridged spreader, coat a manageable area of floor in PVA floor adhesive.

2 Apply wood blocks to the adhesive. Use a length of timber laid across the blocks to check that they all lie flush. Repeat until the floor is covered. Seal the floor with two or three coats of varnish, sanding between coats.

Above: You can make up lots of different patterns. The example here would be easy to do.

Above: Classic herringbone presents problems at the edges if the room is not perfectly square but could be combined with a simpler pattern around the outside.

FLOATING WOODEN FLOORING

Wood-strip flooring is one of the best ways of creating instant elegance. It comes in a huge variety of finishes and lengths, so you can combine different woods without any major laying and fitting difficulties. Once you have grasped the principles of how to lay wood-strip, you can work out many different ways of laying it. The main photograph shows walnut interspersed with wide, light-coloured maple boards. Alternatively, choose just one wood and lay it in different patterns. Wood-strip flooring is available in various types; the ones used here have ingenious metal clips that hold adjacent strips together. A wide range of wood varieties is to be found. Laminated types are generally pre-finished but others need to be sealed once they have been laid.

YOU WILL NEED
- cushioned underlay (if necessary)
- sticky tape
- metal joint clips
- hammer
- wood-strip flooring
- spacers
- wood glue
- saw
- tacks and quadrant beading (optional)
- pencil
- drill with wood bit

2 Prepare all the boards of wood-strip by hammering the special metal joint clips into the groove on the underside of the board, along the tongued edge.

1 Make sure that the subfloor is clean, dry and level. Then unroll the special cushioned underlay, if using, across the floor, taping one end to keep it in place.

3 Lay the first length, clips towards you, against the walls, using spacers to create an expansion gap next to the wall. Glue the ends of butt-jointed lengths.

4 Position the second row of boards, tapping them together with a hammer and an offcut, so that the clips on the first row engage in the groove of the second.

6 Insert some protective packing against the wall before levering the strip into place. Tamp it down level with a hammer and protect the floor with a board offcut.

8 To fit a board around a pipe, mark its position and drill a suitably sized hole. Then cut out a tapered wedge, which can be glued back after fitting the board.

5 The last board is fitted without clips. Cut it to width, allowing for the spacers, as in step 3 and apply adhesive along its grooved edge.

7 Replace the skirtings or tack lengths of quadrant beading to hide the expansion gap; make sure the skirting fits tightly against the floor.

Above: If you want to vary the pattern of the flooring in the centre of the room, as in the main photograph, lay your central boards at right angles to the boards around the outside, if the tongue-and-grooving permits. Three walnut boards followed by a maple board are used here.

COLOUR-WASHED PARQUET

Herringbone patterns on floors give instant classical elegance, suggestive of the wonderful dark oak parquet floors found in the halls and ballrooms of large old houses. However, a younger, freer look is often wanted, yet with all the interest of the old floors; the introduction of a pale, soft colour lifts gloomy dark wood into the realms of light Atlantic beach houses or modern Swedish homes. To keep the interest of the grain of the wood running in different directions, paint each individual piece separately; this can be further enhanced by subtle changes of colour. If you are lucky enough to have a herringbone floor already, and can have a certain amount of patience, masking the blocks individually before painting will give a more professional finish.

YOU WILL NEED

- marine-plywood, cut into manageable lengths
- mitre saw
- tape measure
- sandpaper
- cream matt emulsion paint
- paintbrushes
- blue and white matt emulsion paint
- matt water-based glaze
- lint-free cloth
- PVA floor adhesive
- matt varnish

2 Measure your required length for the herringbone pattern and cut as many as you need for the floor.

1 Make sure the floor is clean, dry and level. Mitre the edges of the marine-ply strips, using a mitre saw. Remember that you must have left- and right-hand mitres in equal numbers.

3 Smooth any rough edges with sandpaper.

4 Undercoat all the boards with a warm cream paint and allow them to dry completely.

5 Mix up at least four variations of your main colour with very little tonal difference between them. Add a little matt water-based glaze to each, to delay the drying time. Thin one of the colours, with water, to make it even more translucent.

6 Paint equal numbers of the boards in each colour.

7 With the cloth, wipe off most of the paint randomly while it is still wet, so that the undercoat shows through. Wipe in the direction of the grain of the wood.

8 For an even more weathered look, sand some areas of some boards; this will give contrast when the floor is down. Lay the floor following the instructions for the Parquet project. Seal the whole floor with two coats of varnish.

Opposite: Give a wholly contemporary interpretation to traditional parquet flooring by colour-washing the blocks individually. There is scope here for matching the floor to your decorative scheme in a more subtle and imaginative way than with a straightforward painted floor.

POP-ART STYLE FLOOR

Much inspiration is to be gleaned from the pop artists of this century, with their whimsical approach to art. These naïve shapes painted on a large surface make use of the pop-art conventions of boldness and simplicity, with multiple repetitions of strong images rather than intricate busyness. Slightly discordant colours – orange and shocking pink in this case – are the most appropriate. This idea is best for a concrete floor.

1 Give the floor two coats of white emulsion, to ensure that the colours of the design ring bright and true.

2 Measure and draw out your design. Mask off the border, which needs to be crisply painted. Do the same along the outside of the star.

3 Paint the star, then fill in the area inside the border; masking may not be necessary for this as a little white space between the star and border and background makes it look as though silk-screening has been used – a technique common in pop art. Seal the floor with diluted PVA glue or acrylic varnish.

WOOD-GRAIN CHECKERBOARD

Checkerboards are a recurrent theme for flooring and yet are rarely seen in natural wood. If you are starting from a concrete or wooden floor, have the new floor covering cut into squares of the size you want and either screw them in place or stick them down. If your floor is already covered in sheets of plywood, MDF or hardboard, mark a checkerboard pattern, ignoring the natural joins. Woodgraining doesn't have to done painstakingly carefully: you can alter the effect produced in the oil paint until it starts to dry. Obtain some reference for the wood effect: we used oak, grained to resemble wood treated in different ways, half "polished" and half "rough-sawn and sand-blasted". You could also use two different wood effects, such as walnut and maple.

YOU WILL NEED
- ◆ pencil
- ◆ tape measure
- ◆ long ruler or straight edge
- ◆ masking tape
- ◆ 2 cream oil-based eggshell paints
- ◆ paintbrushes
- ◆ wood reference
- ◆ artist's oil paints to match wood reference
- ◆ oil-based scumble or glaze
- ◆ white spirit
- ◆ dry-graining brush
- ◆ graining comb
- ◆ satin varnish
- ◆ soft cloth
- ◆ non-slip polish (optional)

1 Make sure the surface is perfectly smooth, then mark off into checkerboard squares, if necessary. Edge alternate squares with strips of masking tape.

2 Using two different cream eggshell paints, paint alternate squares.

3 Mix the oil colours into the glaze, to match the wood reference. Thin with white spirit, if necessary. For the "lighter" squares, brush on the glaze, in the direction you want the "grain" to appear to run, leaving the brush marks visible.

4 Add random strokes.

5 After a few minutes, drag a dry-graining brush over to give the grain.

6 Using a darker oil paint and a fine artist's brush, gently draw in the chevrons of the wood grain.

7 Soften with a brush, adding paint thinner if the paint has dried.

8 For the "darker" squares, repeat step 2.

9 Then repeat step 4, using a graining comb rather than a dry-graining brush, so the grain looks wider.

10 Paint on more noticeable chevrons in the same way, following the grain.

11 Soften the effect, using the graining comb before the brush. Apply two coats of satin varnish and allow to dry. If you like, burnish with a little non-slip polish.

MDF ROUTED

Black cork tiles over the whole floor in this room were too severe, but when the middle section of the room was treated to this wonderful soapstone effect, they became an important part of the overall grand gesture. The cork tiles in the centre were replaced with a large piece of MDF, to which an intricate maze pattern was applied. This could simply have been painted on to plywood or MDF as a two-dimensional effect, but here the surface has been enhanced by routing the maze pattern (take it to a local joiner; routing really isn't for the inexperienced) and then painted to create a soapstone effect. You could also imitate slate, by using a wave formation and the black leading used for cleaning cast-iron fireplaces and grates.

YOU WILL NEED
- ◆ paper
- ◆ pencil
- ◆ MDF sheet
- ◆ plastic wood or wood filler, if necessary
- ◆ fine-grade sandpaper
- ◆ matt emulsion paint: white, dark grey and mid-grey
- ◆ paintbrushes
- ◆ wax candle
- ◆ scraper
- ◆ softening brush
- ◆ matt varnish

1 Plan your design on paper, using this picture as a guide. Draw it on to the sheet of MDF. Take it to a joiner to be routed and ask them to fix it in place on your floor. On an existing floor, draw the maze on the floor directly and ask a joiner to do the routing *in situ*.

2 Fill any damage with plastic wood or wood filler, following the manufacturer's instructions. Don't try to achieve a perfectly flush surface at this stage. Leave to dry.

3 When dry, gently sand until you have a level surface.

4 Paint the whole surface white and allow it to dry.

7 Scrape off most of the candle wax, using a scraper.

10 Apply white paint with a dry softening brush, to soften the whole effect. Seal with matt varnish. If you are surrounding the MDF with cork tiles, lay them at the end and butt them up to the edges neatly.

5 Paint over the whole surface of the floor in dark grey.

8 Follow this with a mid-grey coat.

6 Apply a generous coating of wax using a candle, with circular movements.

9 Apply another coat of wax. Scrape off the wax, using a scraper.

Opposite: Captivate your friends with this maze-patterned floor. The paint effect simulates soapstone but without the coldness or weight of that material.

CHECKED DOOR MATS

Floor mats are easy and cheap to come by and you can often cut them without the edges fraying. They come in many finishes, some even incorporating words or pictures, and all in manageable rectangles.

When these very textured grey polypropylene mats are arranged with the pile running in different directions, a checkerboard effect is achieved or a combination of colours could be funky.

YOU WILL NEED
- ◆ string
- ◆ white crayon or chalk
- ◆ tape measure
- ◆ grey polypropylene door mats
- ◆ long metal ruler or straight edge
- ◆ craft knife
- ◆ notched spreader
- ◆ floor adhesive

1 Use strings to find the room's centre (*see Techniques*) and mark with a cross. If possible, link the opposite pairs of walls. Measure the floor and work out how many floor mats you will need. Mark the cuts with a white crayon or chalk on the reverse of the floor mats.

2 If the mats are of carpet quality, score along the lines before cutting with the craft knife. Then cut the mats to size.

3 Using a notched spreader, apply floor adhesive to the floor.

4 Starting at the centre, carefully lay the mats in position, remembering that, for the check effect shown here, you need to alternate the weaves.

STENCILLED HARDBOARD

Damaged or irregular floors are frequently covered in hardboard and you may feel that this hard surface is more in keeping if you have adopted a modernist, minimalist approach to decorating. In most cases, if you discover hardboard in mint condition, it is not wise to lift it: as it is probably hiding some horror below. However, with several coats of varnish, hardboard has a natural patina of its own, which is very appealing and works as a neutral background as well as does a wooden floor. Introduce added interest by using stencils, which here mimic a rather fifties-style rug, though the brown hardboard would suit different colours. The contrast of black or white works well; choose a bold, non-figurative pattern.

YOU WILL NEED

- pencil
- paper
- black water-based paint
- paintbrushes
- metal ruler or straight edge
- masking tape
- self-healing cutting mat
- acetate sheet
- craft knife
- pin
- stencil brush
- lint-free cloth or fine-grade sandpaper, if necessary
- eraser
- gloss varnish

1 Draw the border motif to the desired size on paper, using the template at the back of the book.

2 Photocopy the design and make sure that the repeat works, by placing several sheets together.

3 Work out a right-angled section for the corners. Make sure it ties in neatly with the repeat on both sides.

4 Black in the design and photocopy it. Decide how far in from the edges of the room the border will be. Now lay the photcopies around the floor, to ensure that your design will fit pleasingly, and experiment until you have an effect you are happy with.

5 With pencil, mark the outer edge of your border on the floor (in the photograph, this is about 13cm/5½in from the edge of the room).

6 Draw out pencil guidelines for your border all round the room.

7 Stick one of the photocopies, with masking tape, to the cutting mat. Tape the acetate over it.

8 Using the steel ruler and holding the knife at an angle, carefully cut out the stencil. To help get neat, sharp corners, make a pin prick just at the corner first; this also helps to prevent you from cutting too far.

9 With masking tape, attach the stencil to the hardboard, lining it up with your guidelines.

10 Using a stencil brush, stipple in the neat black triangles, making sure that the paint does not seep under the stencil.

11 Lift up the stencil and re-position it for the next section. Remember to make sure the underside of the stencil is clear of paint. If you need to mask certain areas of the stencil so that you continue the repeat when working the corners, do this with a piece of paper held firmly in place with masking tape.

12 If you make a mistake or slightly smudge the stencilling, either quickly rub it clean with a damp cloth or, if the surface is more porous, very gently sand away the paint when dry. Finally, remove the pencil guidelines with an eraser and seal the floor with at least two coats of varnish, paying particular attention to the stencilled areas.

Right: Hardboard floors are practical but not usually glamorous; however, hardboard can gain its own natural patina with layers of varnish and the addition of a bold, graphic stencilled border enhances the earthy and rugged feel of the floor, to create a really strong impact.

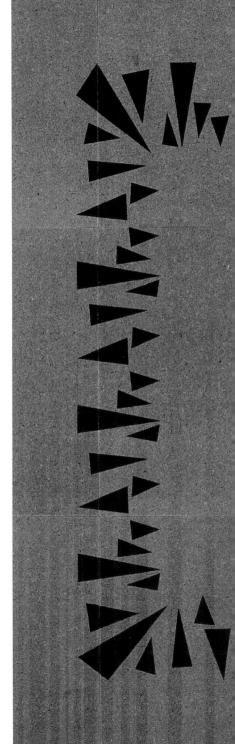

RUBBER MATS

Available from rubber manufacturers, this rubber safety matting is valued for its non-slip and protective qualities, and, since it is waterproof, it is particularly useful in, say, a shower room. It comes on a roller in a broad spectrum of colours, widths and textures, from specialist shops. It doesn't fray and will happily absorb any lumps or strange joins in a floor. Clean and seal the matting with a silicone spray polish.

YOU WILL NEED

- ◆ 2 types of rubber safety mat
- ◆ tape measure
- ◆ metal rule or straight edge
- ◆ craft knife
- ◆ Pirelli rubber tiles in different patterns
- ◆ rubber contact adhesive
- ◆ WD-40 or silicone spray

1 Measure the floor and the rubber matting and carefully trim the long runners to size.

2 For the corners, cut four squares. Divide these diagonally and make four squares by placing two triangles together, with the grooves running across and top to bottom. Position these and the runners around the edge of the room.

3 Cut pieces from the other matting to fit the central section. Cut the tiles into squares, then cut holes in the mat at regular intervals to take the squares.

4 Secure all the pieces with rubber adhesive, applied to both surfaces. Spray with WD-40 or silicone spray.

DISTRESSED FLOORBOARDS

Wooden floors are often appealing because of their subtle variations of colour that improve with age. Your wooden floors may not be in a great state to begin with, though, or may look uninteresting, and you don't really want to wait for the years to work their magic naturally. Wood stains can help to imitate that look in only a few hours. The look of driftwood or weathered teak or other hardwood decking, such as is found in beach houses, is the aim. Achieve the outdoor look using three different wood dyes and a wash of white emulsion, diluted almost to water. This technique would give a bleached effect to any wood stain; for example, over a warm mahogany, which would otherwise be quite dark, a wash of cream or white instantly gives the faded look of maturity.

YOU WILL NEED
- nail punch
- hammer
- power sander and fine-grade sandpaper
- wire brush
- 3 different wood stains of the same make
- lint-free cloth or paintbrushes
- rubber gloves
- white or cream emulsion paint
- dry cloth
- matt polyurethane floor varnish

1 It's important that floors have no sharp or protruding nails and so on, so knock in any you find with a nail punch before you begin (*see Techniques*). Remove old paint spills using a sander. Remember to change the sandpaper frequently, or you will damage the rubber seal of the sander.

2 Brush the boards with a wire brush, along the direction of the grain, with the occasional cross stroke to give a distressed effect.

3 Experiment with the stains, mixing colours together – a little should go a long way. Use scrap wood, to test the effect before you commit yourself.

4 With either a lint-free cloth or a brush, apply the stain. This will stain anything porous, so wear rubber gloves and old clothes.

5 Start by applying quite a generous quantity of stain but rub most of the surplus off. Don't stop till you've finished the floor or there will be a definite line; keep the joins between areas random and avoid overlapping parallel bands of stain.

6 It's better to do one thin coat all over and then go back to apply further coats, perhaps working the stain into knots or grooves with a brush, to give an uneven, weathered look.

7 While this is still wet, brush on a wash of the diluted white or cream paint, about one part emulsion to four parts water.

8 Using a dry cloth, rub off surplus or apply more until you have the effect you want.

9 Apply two coats of clear varnish, sanding very lightly between coats.

GLOSSY TONGUE-AND-GROOVE

Tongued-and-grooved boards look wonderful with a gleaming shine; it has to be one of the most dynamic uplifts you can bring to a room. Gloss paint or floor paint is wonderfully durable and easily renewed, if it's ever damaged. Use this floor in a room with a large window, if you can, and watch the dramatic effect of the sun streaming in and highlighting the gloss. Gloss paint shows up detail, so it was a natural choice for these brand-new tongued-and-grooved boards but, if you like the effect of the dramatic colour but have a an old, beaten-up floor, a matt finish would be more forgiving. To lay a new floor of this type, a perfectly smooth and level subfloor, such as hardboard, chipboard or marine-plywood, is vital (see Techniques for how to lay these).

YOU WILL NEED

- ◆ tongued-and-grooved boards
- ◆ hammer
- ◆ drill, with pilot drill bit
- ◆ flooring pins
- ◆ pin hammer
- ◆ nail punch
- ◆ power sander, with coarse-, medium- and fine-grade sandpaper
- ◆ undercoat paint
- ◆ paintbrushes
- ◆ high-gloss floor paint

1 Slot the tongued-and-grooved boards together and, using an offcut to protect the exposed tongue, tap the next board into place until it fits tightly. If the boards are warped, pin one end first and work along the board; in this way you will be able to straighten out the warp.

2 To prevent the tongues from splitting, pre-drill pilot holes.

3 Tap pins in gently, using a pin hammer, at a slight angle back towards the boards.

4 Punch the pins in with a nail punch so the next board can butt up.

5 When the floor is laid, and before finishing it, sand the floor, first with a coarse-grade sandpaper and then with medium-grade and finally with fine-grade. Always sand in line with the wood grain. With long, even strokes, running in line with the boards, undercoat the floor. Leave to dry.

6 Lightly sand the whole floor again, to make it smoother. Finally, paint the whole floor with your chosen gloss paint.

Right: Tongued-and-grooved boards are more often associated with wainscotting in country-style kitchens but they make an easily-laid flooring, too. A high-gloss, intensely coloured finish is here used to stunning effect in a contemporary setting.

SHEET-METAL TREAD MATS

Sheet-metal tread plates are a very versatile flooring. They may be painted but look dazzling left in their natural state. Sheet-metal wholesalers offer a wide range of metals, such as copper, zinc and so on, and will cut the sheets to size. They can be laid on concrete or on a subfloor of hardboard, chipboard or marine-plywood (see Techniques).

YOU WILL NEED
- wood scrap
- drill, with metal pilot drill bit, and wood drill bit, if necessary
- sheet-metal tread mats
- metal file
- wood screws, if necessary
- screwdriver
- floor adhesive, if necessary

1 Using a metal file, file away any rough edges, being careful not to create file marks on the visible top surface of the sheets.

2 Using a small piece of wood as a rest and a metal pilot drill bit, drill holes in every corner of the mats and at every 12in/20cm along the sides, depending on the size of the sheets.

3 If you're laying metal sheets on a wooden floor, screw through the holes in the metal into the wood surface with wood screws.

4 Butt up the sheets together and continue screwing them to the floor. If you have a concrete floor, these sheets can be glued directly in place. To finish, fit metal or wooden quadrant beading around the edges.

GOLD PAINT AND SCRIM FLOOR

In the past, only travellers to far-flung countries could furnish their homes with exotic tables, fabrics, pots and statues, but today such ethnic treasures are widely available and sometimes require a more dramatic backdrop than subtle monotones.

Gold, copper and silver strike a note of flamboyance, but texture is also needed if the scheme is to be a rich foil for your possessions. Builders' scrim, used to reinforce plaster, fits the bill. It gives a wonderful surface that traps different amounts of gold and copper, creating the effect of beaten metal. It allows for a play of patterns such as tartans and checks that would otherwise be difficult to regulate.

As with all exotic finishes, the delight here lies more in the instant transformation than in practicality.

YOU WILL NEED

- ◆ tape measure
- ◆ pencil
- ◆ paper and ruler
- ◆ power sander, with fine-grade sandpaper
- ◆ builders' scrim
- ◆ scissors
- ◆ wide paintbrush
- ◆ PVA glue
- ◆ oil-based gold paint
- ◆ copper powder paint
- ◆ heavy-duty floor varnish

1 Measure your floor. Taking into account the width of the scrim, plan your design on paper first, to make sure that your chosen tartan or check repeat doesn't leave you with an awkward half line at the edges of the room.

2 You need a smooth, flat surface to work on. If necessary, lay a marine-plywood or hardboard floor (*see Techniques*). Lightly sand the floor to make sure it's perfectly flat.

3 Cut the lengths of scrim, beginning with the longest, and lay it to your chosen pattern. Conceal joins at points where two lengths cross over, hiding the join underneath, and over-lapping the ends by at least 15cm/6in.

4 Stick the scrim down with PVA glue. Brush out any glue that soaks through to the top to hold the scrim firmly. Don't worry if you spread glue outside the area of the scrim. Pencil in a few guidelines and put a weight on the other end of the scrim to keep it straight.

6 Paint on the gold paint with the wide brush, covering the whole floor. If using an oil-based paint, ensure you have plenty of ventilation in the room. Allow to dry.

8 Apply at least two coats of heavy-duty floor varnish to seal.

5 Dilute the PVA with water and coat the whole floor, going over the stuck-down scrim as well. This seals the floor and forms a key for the gold paint.

7 Dust the copper powder paint over the scrim, allowing it to be trapped by the mesh surface.

LINOLEUM IN 3-D PATTERNS

Linoleum now comes in many thicknesses, colours and patterns and while it doesn't quite have the appeal of a beautiful classical floor, by cutting it into trompe l'oeil *patterns and playing with slight colour variations you can create quite grand effects. Aside from the fact that lino is hard-wearing, water-resistant and probably one of the least expensive floor coverings, given this dramatic treatment, it can become the centrepiece of any hall, kitchen or bathroom that is bare of furnishings most of the time. Rolls of lino and floor adhesive were used in this project but you could also use self-glued tiles to make a floor reminiscent of a Venetian palazzo. For this technique you need patience, exact templates and the kind of mind that adores jigsaw puzzles.*

YOU WILL NEED

- ◆ power sander, with fine-grade sandpaper
- ◆ tape measure
- ◆ pencil
- ◆ paper
- ◆ ruler
- ◆ long metal ruler or straight edge
- ◆ linoleum rolls in different colours
- ◆ hardboard sheet
- ◆ saw
- ◆ craft knife
- ◆ contact floor adhesive

2 Having made sure no nail heads are exposed, lightly sand the floor, to make sure it's perfectly flat.

1 You need a smooth, flat surface on which to apply the lino. If necessary, lay a marine-plywood or hardwood floor (*see Techniques*).

3 Measure your floor. To ensure a good fit, it's very important to work out your pattern on paper first, using the template at the back of the book.

4 Draw grid lines on the floor as a guide when the laying the lino shapes.

5 Using a piece of hardboard, draw each of the pattern shapes and cut them out carefully with a saw.

6 Use these templates to cut out the lino shapes. Remember that, unlike carpet tiles, lino isn't very forgiving and accuracy is all-important.

7 Try out your pattern in pieces of lino and see if any need trimming. If necessary, number them on the back to help you fit them together.

8 Using contact adhesive, apply glue to the floor and the backs of the tiles and fit them in place; you cannot adjust them once they are laid.

Opposite: Reminiscent of the cunning drawings of Escher, this eye-deceiving, "three-dimensional" design is executed in shapes cut from linoleum. You are limited only by your own imagination in using this technique to produce individual masterpieces.

FAKE-FUR ANIMAL-SKIN RUG

Giving a new meaning to a baby on a sheep-skin rug, this fun idea could be scaled up for a full-size rug. Rather than making a classical bear- or lion-skin rug, be more tongue-in-cheek, with shapes such as prehistoric animals or farm animals. Fake furs now come in bright colours, so you could take the concept even further from reality; mix up shapes and patterns.

YOU WILL NEED

◆ large tissue paper sheet
◆ pencil
◆ long ruler
◆ dressmaker's pins
◆ fake fur fabric
◆ scissors
◆ thick felt
◆ pinking shears
◆ iron-on hemming strip and iron, or sewing machine or sewing needle and matching thread

1 Draw a line down the middle of the paper, then draw half the bear shape on one side, following the template at the back of the book. Fold in half along the line and cut out the shape.

2 Enlarge the paper pattern to size then pin it to your fur fabric

3 Cut your shape out and then cut the shape out again from the felt, using pinking shears. Include a 6cm/2½in allowance all round.

4 Stick the wrong side of the fur shape to the right side of the felt shape with the hemming strip. Alternatively, either machine or slip stitch the two fabrics together.

VERMEER-STYLE MARBLE

You may be faced with a hardboard floor and long for the grandeur and impact of a marble one. Marbling is relatively easy to do. A wonderfully strong pattern is used here, taken from Vermeer's Old Master paintings. You may choose to do a simple checkerboard or behave as if you had a huge slab of marble – a wildly expensive choice if it was real marble. Find a small piece of marble as reference, as there is such a variety of marbles to choose from and its realistic effect is dependent on understanding how the veins of your particular marble run. This technique of flooring is not suitable for anywhere where there is a lot of moisture as, for example, a bathroom, but a marbled dining room could also look amazing.

YOU WILL NEED

- ◆ tape measure
- ◆ paper
- ◆ pencil
- ◆ ruler
- ◆ black felt-tipped pen
- ◆ white undercoat paint
- ◆ paint roller
- ◆ long straight edge, e.g. skirting length
- ◆ oil-based glaze
- ◆ artist's oil colours: light and dark grey, black and silver
- ◆ paintbrushes
- ◆ lint-free cloth
- ◆ bird's feather or quill
- ◆ softening brush
- ◆ dry cloth
- ◆ fine artist's brush
- ◆ black oil-based eggshell paint
- ◆ white spirit
- ◆ matt varnish

1 Measure your room, then draw a scale plan and a grid on it, using the template at the back of the book.

2 Fill in your design, starting from the middle point of the floor and working out to the edges.

3 You need a very flat surface, such as hardboard or marine-plywood (*see Techniques*). Undercoat the floor with a couple of coats of white paint.

5 Add a little grey oil paint to the glaze and apply it very thinly, using a brush, to all the squares which don't have black dots and will therefore be white "marble".

7 With a lint-free cloth, soften the glaze while it is still wet.

4 Draw the design on the floor in pencil. Put a blob of black paint in each square that is going to be painted black.

6 Add more colour to the glaze, by dotting small amounts of oil paint directly on to your brush. Apply selectively to some areas.

8 Take a bird's feather or quill, dipped into a mixture of black paint thinned with a little glaze, and gently draw across the surface, to simulate the veins.

9 Use the softening brush to blur the outlines of the veining and blend them with the background. Wipe the brush regularly on a dry cloth to avoid smudges.

10 With a fine artist's brush, further soften the effect by adding white spirit, which will dissipate the lines. You can also add more colour or a second colour, but remember to soften it again.

11 Clean up the edges of the pencil squares with the corner of dry cloth.

12 Carefully fill in the black squares indicated by the black dots.

13 Using a little grey or silver paint, applied directly on to a brush dampened with white spirit, soften the black to look like slate, in swirling motions. Finally, give the floor several coats of varnish.

Opposite: Marbling is one of the most dramatic paint effects but it isn't too difficult to do if you take the stages steadily. If you have always dreamed of living in a palazzo but have had to settle for a flat, create the cool, tranquil, dreamy atmosphere of marbled-floor luxury for yourself.

PATCHWORK CERAMIC TILES

Bathrooms, shower rooms and kitchens are often thought of as utility rooms, and their floorings are correspondingly spartan.

But the wide range of ceramic tiles now available enables you to achieve stunning good looks without sacrificing practicality. Here we opted for stylish blue tiles in the same colour range accented by deep indigo.

1 Draw a grid on the floor for the tiles (*see Techniques*).

2 Spread some adhesive on the floor, using the spreader. As you lay the tiles use spacers to ensure even gaps between them. Use a straight-edge to check all the tiles are horizontal and level. Use a squeegee to spread grout over the tiles and fill all the join lines.

3 Wipe off the surplus grout with a damp sponge before it dries.

4 Buff with a dry cloth when the grout has hardened, then smooth the grout with the piece of dowel.

MATERIALS

As floors are often made of heavy-duty materials, some of the projects require specialist tools, such as a power sander and tile cutters. These can be hired on a daily basis from any good DIY shop.

Your basic tool kit should include an electric drill, screwdriver, tape measure, hammer, a long straight edge (preferably metal), sharp scissors, a craft knife and spare blades, pliers, masking tape, a range of different types of sandpaper and a range of paintbrushes.

There are many different adhesives available on the market for sticking down floor surfaces. Consult your local supplier about the surface you are planning to lay and what type of glue you should use. If you are working with a solvent-based glue, follow the safety instructions on the packaging and make sure the area you are working in is well-ventilated.

Varnishes are used to protect paintwork from wear and tear. As with paints, varnishes come in both oil and water-based varieties and matt, satin or gloss finishes. If you have used an oil-based paint on your floor, you must use an oil-based varnish to cover it. Equally if you have used water-based paint then use a water-based varnish. You can use a plain or tinted varnish depending on the effect you wish to create. When applying the varnish always use a clean brush that has not been used for the paintwork.

At all times safety precautions should be followed. You should never cut towards yourself when using sharp cutting tools; protective clothing should be worn when working with solvent-based materials; great care should be taken when working with heavy machinery.

Right: Measuring tape (1); carpet tiles cut to shape (2); hammer (3); craft knife (4); mirror head screws (5); glue sticks to go in a glue gun (6); builders' scrim (7); wire brush (8); nail punch (9); stencil brush (10); panel pins (11); scraper (12); saw (13); floorboard nails (14); ceramic floor tiles (15); parquet flooring blocks (16); domes of silence (17).

TECHNIQUES

For nearly all the projects in this book you must work on a clean, flat surface such as hardboard, marine-plywood or sanded floorboards. Shown here are a few basic guidelines on floor-surface preparation. If you are in any doubt about your ability to carry out these instructions then ask a professional to help you.

Securing loose floorboards

For suspended wooden floors (boards laid over floor joists), start by lifting the old floor covering, if any, and checking that all the boards are securely fixed to their joists, and that they are reasonably flat and level. Loose boards will creak annoyingly when walked on and raised edges or pronounced warping may show as lines through the new floor covering.

Use either cut nails or large, oval-headed nails to secure loose boards. When driving them near known pipe or cable runs, take care not to pierce these; it is best to drive the new nails as close to existing nail positions as possible, for safety.

YOU WILL NEED

- ◆ nail punch
- ◆ hammer
- ◆ drill, with wood pilot drill bit
- ◆ wood screws
- ◆ screwdriver

1 Drive in any nails that have lifted due to warping or twisting on the floorboards and then recess their heads slightly, using a nail punch.

2 If nails won't hold the floorboards flat against the joist, drill pilot and clearance holes and use wood screws to secure the boards firmly in place.

Laying hardboard or marine-plywood

Covering existing boards with a hardboard or marine-plywood underlay is an alternative to floor sanding as a way of ensuring a smooth, flat surface, ideal for more decorative floor coverings or for embellishing in its own right. Lay the boards in rows, with joints staggered from row to row, and pin them down with hardboard pins, driven in at 15cm/6in intervals. Lay separate strips above where you know there are pipe runs.

If you're going to lay glazed ceramic or quarry tiles on a suspended wooden floor, put down exterior-grade plywood to support their weight.

Y O U   W I L L   N E E D

◆ nail punch

◆ hammer

◆ hardboard pins

◆ tack hammer

1 If hardboard sheets are used as an underlay for a new floor covering, start by punching in any raised nail heads all over the floor with a nail punch.

2 Nail the hardboard sheets to the floorboards at 15cm/6in intervals along the edges and at 30cm/12in intervals across the face of the sheet.

Sanding floorboards

Where old floor boards are very uneven, or you plan to leave them exposed but they are badly stained and marked, hire a floor-sanding machine. This resembles a cylinder lawnmower, with a drum to which sheets of sandpaper are fitted. A bag at the rear collects the sawdust; however, always wear a face mask when sanding floors. Also hire a smaller disc or belt sander for finishing off the edges.

If necessary, drive any visible nail heads below the surface. Start sanding with coarse-grade paper at 45° to the direction of the floor boards; then use medium and fine-grade paper in turn, with the machine running parallel to the boards. Use the disc or belt sander to tackle the perimeter of the room, where the large sander can't reach.

Y O U   W I L L   N E E D

◆ floor sander, with coarse-, medium- and fine-grade sandpaper

◆ smaller disc or belt sander

◆ scraper

◆ sandpaper and sanding block

1 Use a floor sander to smooth and strip old floorboards. Drape the flex over one shoulder and raise the drum before starting the machine.

2 Run the machine at 45° to the direction of the floor boards and with coarse-grade sandpaper fitted, first in one direction and then at right angles to the original passes.

3 Switch to a medium-grade sandpaper and run the sander back and forth, parallel with the grain of the boards. Finish off with fine-grade sandpaper.

4 Use a smaller disc or belt sander to strip areas close to the skirtings and door thresholds, where the larger drum sander can't reach.

5 Use a scraper to remove paint or varnish from inaccessible areas, such as around pipes. Then sand the stripped areas smooth by hand.

Laying chipboard

You can level and insulate a concrete floor by laying a floating floor of chipboard over it. This provides an ideal subfloor for many of the projects described in this book.

YOU WILL NEED
- heavy-duty polythene sheets
- sticky tape
- 2.5cm/1in polystyrene insulation boards
- tongued-and-grooved flooring-grade chipboard panels

1 Lay the polythene sheets.

2 Tape the sheet to the walls. Butt-joint the boards all over the floor.

3 Cut the chipboard to fit and lay it over the insulation boards.

Setting out tiled floors

Like tiled walls, tiled floors need careful setting-out if the end result is to look neat and professional. This is especially important with glazed ceramic and quarry tiles and also patterned vinyl and lino tiles; it matters rather less with plain vinyl and cork tiles, where the joins between the tiles are practically invisible.

Fortunately, the necessary setting-out is much easier with floor tiles than wall tiles, since you can dry-lay the tiles on the floor surface and move them around until you find a starting point that gives the best arrangement, with cut border tiles of approximately equal size around the perimeter of the room. In a regularly shaped room, start by finding the actual centre of the floor, by linking the midpoints of opposite pairs of walls, with string lines. In an irregularly shaped room, place string lines so that they avoid obstructions, and then link the midpoints of opposite pairs of strings, to find the room's centre. Now dry-lay rows of tiles out towards the walls, in each direction, remembering to allow for the joint thickness, if

appropriate, to see how many whole tiles will fit in and to check whether this starting point results in over-narrow border tiles or awkward cuts against obstacles. Move the rows slightly to improve the fit, if necessary, and then chalk the string lines and snap them against the floor surface, to mark the starting point.

1 In a regularly shaped room, find the room's centre by linking the midpoints of opposite walls with string lines.

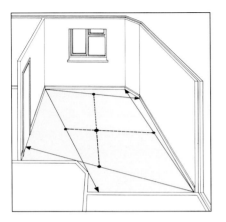

2 In an irregularly shaped room, use string lines that avoid obstacles and link the midpoints of these, as shown, to find the centre point.

3 To ensure that tiles will be laid square to the door threshold, place a string line at right angles to it, across the room to the opposite wall.

4 Place a second string line at right angles to the first, so that it passes through the room's centre point.

5 Place a third string line at right angles to the second, again passing though the centre point, to complete the laying guide.

6 Dry-lay rows of tiles out from the centre of the room towards the walls, allowing for the joint width between tiles as appropriate, to check the width of the border tiles and the fit around the obstacles.

7 Adjust the string lines to get the best possible fit, chalk them and snap them against the floor to make the laying guidelines.

Laying ceramic floor tiles

Both glazed ceramic and quarry tiles can be laid directly over a concrete floor, as long as it is sound and dry. They can also be laid on a suspended timber floor, if it is strong enough to support the extra weight (check with a building surveyor). In this case, cover the floorboards with exterior-grade plywood, screwed down or secured with annular nails (ringed flooring nails) to prevent it from lifting; this will provide a stable, level base for the tiles.

Glazed ceramic floor tiles are laid with specially formulated adhesive, which should be of a waterproof type in bathrooms and of a flexible type if you're tiling on a suspended floor. Quarry and terracotta tiles are laid on mortar, over a solid concrete floor, and in thick-bed tile adhesive over plywood.

Lift old floor coverings before laying ceramic or quarry tiles, but if a solid floor is covered with well-bonded vinyl or cork tiles, leave these left in place and tile over them, using tile adhesive. First remove any wax polish on them.

Set out the floor as described on the previous spread but transfer the starting point to the corner of the room farthest from the door, once the setting-out has been completed.

Remember to take off and shorten any room doors before laying floor tiles; and remove enough to allow the door to clear both the plywood underlay and the new tiles.

YOU WILL NEED

- ◆ pencil
- ◆ tiles
- ◆ lengths of wood
- ◆ pins
- ◆ tile adhesive
- ◆ notched spreader
- ◆ tile spacers
- ◆ large nail
- ◆ tile cutter
- ◆ squeegee
- ◆ grout
- ◆ damp sponge
- ◆ dowel scrap
- ◆ clean, dry, soft, lint-free cloth

1 Use a pencil and one of the tiles to mark up lengths of wood to use as a tiling guide. Allow for the width of the tile spacers. Pin tiling guides to the floor in the corner of the room, at right angles to each other; then spread some adhesive on the floor, with a notched spreader.

2 Put the first tile in the angle between the tiling guides, butting it tightly against them and pressing it down firmly into the adhesive bed.

3 As the tiles are laid, use tile spacers to ensure an even gap between them. Use a straight edge to check that all the tiles are horizontal and level.

5 Cut the tile and fill the border gap. Continue to cut pieces from the offcut to fill the gap.

7 Use a piece of dowel or similar implement to smooth the grout lines, then buff the tiles with a clean cloth.

4 To cut border tiles, lay a whole tile over a tile laid against the tiling guide, butt another against the skirting board and mark its edge on the tile underneath with a nail.

6 Use a squeegee to spread grout over the tiles and fill all the joint lines. Wipe excess adhesive from the surface of the tiles with a damp sponge.

TEMPLATES

Photocopy montage

Fake-fur animal skin rug

Linoleum 3-D in patterns

Stencilled hardboard

INDEX